Ripples

Ripples: A Memoir of Reflection
Copyright © 2020; 2017 by Diana LéGere

Published by Arabelle Publishing, LLC.
PO Box 2841
Chesterfield, VA 23832

The names and characteristics of these stories have been changed to protect the privacy of the individuals. The dialogue in this story is not meant to be a word-for-word transcript, but a creative account based on actual events in the life of the author.

Unless otherwise noted, Scripture is taken from the New King James Version®. Copyright © 1982 by Thomas Nelson. Used by permission. All rights reserved.

Cover and interior design by Lance Buckley
Cover photo © Can Stock Photo Inc.

ISBN 978-0-9979126-54
Library of Congress Number: 2019942293

Printed in the USA.

Praise for Ripples

〰〰〰

I thoroughly enjoyed reading Diana's new book. She is an excellent writer, and I could see myself dipping my toes in the lake as she did as a child. She pulls you in as each chapter tells you a story of her life. In her introduction, one sentence in particular hit close to home. "Change leads to something good when you have a receptive heart." I highly recommend this book.

SARAH NORKUS, *Author of Broken Together* - Goodreads review

There were three sections that spoke to me on a spiritual level: "Be authentic," "There is nothing God would put into your heart He would not bring to pass," and "What we have is today." For someone who has been yearning for self-reflection and self-discovery, LeGere's words and lessons were inspirational. I am in a period of transition, but I need to be true to myself as I relinquish control and let God guide me. With that being said, I need to seize new opportunities as my heart leads me by God's direction. I gained a greater connection with myself and with God through working my way through LeGere's memoir, and I believe that anyone striving to better understand themselves and/or striving to better understand life's journey will enjoy this book.

K. GREEN - Amazon review

Thoughtful and transparent. Diana shares from the heart even when faced with challenges that didn't always end as she had hoped or expected. Her reflections will give you pause to view your own experiences with a learning point of view. Well written. Good read. Prayers will bring you closer to God in a conversational relationship.

DIANE MERRYMAN - Goodreads review

This is truly a very inspiring and uplifting book for me. I loved how the author Diana described or shared the stories or events in the book. It was if I'm in the same place or scenario with her. Everyone can definitely relate to her stories, and it's so inspiring to read on how God has made a big impact in her life.

SHEILA JORDAN - Goodreads review

Ripples is easy to read and very inspiring! The stories are relatable and make you reflect on your own life. The personal stories make you feel like you are not alone. I love how the chapters are followed by prayers making it easy for the reader to ask God to work in his/her own life. A must read for everyone!

HEATHER PETERSON - Goodreads review

Delightful stories told with a touch of humor dot the pages, and they are followed by enlivening scriptures. Reflectional questions and prayers are also included at the end of each section. They make the insight in the book actionable. Ripples: A Memoir of Reflection by Diana LeGere encourages us to live a less stressful and more meaningful life by inviting God into our lives.

EDITH WAIRIMU - Readers' Favorite

A wonderful find! In our busy, fast-paced world, Ripples gave me permission to slow down and reflect. I found myself responding to the questions unhurriedly and honestly because the author is so transparent. This book is refreshing and powerful in an unassuming way. Before I knew it, I was transported back in time, and nuggets of truth in my life found clarity. And I'm the better for it. Relax, enjoy, and hopefully, you'll take your mask off too.

CAROL GREEN - Goodreads review

For Renee, Michael, and Amanda.
You are the most precious gifts God has ever given me.

Acknowledgements

I am grateful for my parents and siblings, who hold a special place in my heart. As I grow older, I'm convinced memories are priceless, and family is everything.

Introduction

A STONE DROPS

~~~~~

Water calms me. The ocean, a lake, a swimming pool, even a puddle. Gentle ripples carry me off to a peaceful place.

I grew up around ponds and lakes. When the weight of real or imagined tragic events stole my joy, I retreated to water with pen and paper. Sometimes, to write, but often to dip my toes.

Here, my inner child learned to sail through the streams of life with a marked sense of positivity. I lived a wonderful pseudo-life, downplaying everything I perceived as objectionable. A positive thinker is virtuous if grounded. Standing on the rim of truth, my bad habit was telling myself, however bad something seemed, it wasn't *that* bad. It was only a temporary inconvenience. Also, good things weren't *that* good. I was always hoping nobody would notice my feelings didn't match my expression. This avoidance brought me into adulthood, pretending nothing needed fixing. Not my surroundings, and not myself. I had a lot to learn.

First, circumstances don't always need changing. The challenges of life are good teachers. We can fight the learning curve or navigate through the trials. The quicker we master the process, the sooner we find ourselves with a new set of encounters. Sometimes, a blessing to reward and remind us we passed a test. Or, maybe we discover we've been around the mountain, and it's time to retest. I'm tired of retaking tests. I want extra homework and a study partner from the get-go!

My journey has helped me to understand I often made life much harder than it was. I fought against changes. But, change leads to something good when we have a receptive heart.

Time has taught me each life choice has a ripple effect on our lives and those we love. Sometimes, one ripple can last for decades. Those ripples can be a joy to remember, or they can sting like a bee.

✦ I've spent far too many hours anxious of the unknown and everything that scared me. I worried about things that never materialized. Panic over the tiniest thing from a burnt roast to not having money for a roast, to losing a job.

I'm content with less even though my resources have grown. Sometimes, unemployment was the break I needed. Although most often, I didn't appreciate it until I had another job. Every life phase offers new opportunities and prepares us for the future. The hardest step for me was trusting the process. Maybe, you discovered, like me, the best things in life money can't buy. These are things I would buy more of, but they've never been available for purchase. They are gifts free to all who are ready to receive. But we must look for them. They flutter by quickly and we must enjoy them before they are gone.

Ripples remind me to focus on the destination *and* the journey. The cause and effect of each thing we say and do are sometimes hard lessons learned along the way. I've had a few harsh experiences, more than I care to admit. We'd all like at least one retake in our lifetime. That rarely happens. If you're reading this and have had second chances, praise God and never stop thanking Him! The rest of us are putting on our big-girl panties and learning how to get on with our lives.

We crawl before we can walk or run. Even now, I'm often reminded to attach the cart *to* the horse, but I'm always getting ahead of myself. Be eager for nothing. Everything works out in due time. I'm learning not to be in a hurry.

For me, it's hard to slow down. I start one thing, and with lightning speed, I'm ready to climb higher. I have faith I can do more in a year than possible, and I tackle too many projects at once. I'm trying to live now…in the present.

There was a time I rushed through life, making many waves that affected everyone around me. I worried about me far more than necessary. Sometimes, I wasted a lot of energy manipulating my course, never seeing each chapter for its own beauty. Everything has a silver lining. The greatest lesson has been learning to accept that the best action is often to lay back and float. Enjoy each day. Be still. Let the water guide and watch the gentle ripples as you glide along the way. Accept each new day as a beautiful and precious gift. Don't worry about tomorrow. It will take care of itself.

A woman once gave me advice that changed my life. "Be a good learner," she said.

I always fed my ego and wanted to be the teacher. Now, I wonder why it was so important. It's a big responsibility fighting to hold the answer key. If I keep the key or not, I don't have all the answers. There's more growing and learning for me to do. My slogan moving forward is, "What can you teach me?" I'm soaking it in like a sponge.

Often, the youngest teachers will give you the best learning experience. There have been times I've put all my trust in the wrong people and didn't trust the good ones enough. When you wear a mask, it distorts your vision.

I've often pursued the uphill trek that took twice as long, was harder, and often, went nowhere. Imagine packing your vehicle for a vacation and never getting out of the driveway. Fun, right?

Meanwhile, God was always there, waiting. He had it all carved out on level ground if I would follow His lead and get out of my way. Are you done driving, Diana? *Yes.* And, I'm okay with letting go.

I used to remind myself during stressful periods, *this too, shall pass*. True, but on the flip side, it all passes. The difficult times, but also what delights us and makes us smile. Enjoy every moment ... today. Whatever we have will change. Nothing stays the same. But, it's comforting to know, even when defeated, in time we'll be on the upswing again.

Life is always changing. I'm learning to appreciate and look forward to changes and the opportunities they bring. I'm grateful for all the beautiful people and experiences God has brought into my life.

This book has a few memories and thoughts. My perspective has changed over the years. As you read the stories, I hope they inspire you to reflect on "your" reminiscences.

There is space for you to journal, ask yourself questions, and reflect on the ripples in life.

A stone dropped into a lake spreads ripples across the entire surface. Likewise, our actions seep into our circles of influence, often affecting others in ways unknown. Let the surrounding waves in your life be of joy and inspiration.

Diana LéGere
2nd Edition November 2019

Chapter 1

A THANKFUL HEART

~~~~~

Too often, I've succumbed to a false belief that my life was not full. I thought I had little to give, so I held on tight and waited to get. Other times, I gave away the farm, but for the wrong reasons. There was no middle ground.

As an adult, I've enjoyed more material riches than I experienced growing up in the rural northeast. By American standards, our family was poor. I never knew it. Surrounded by woods, pastures, and ponds, the outdoors was our playground and a substitute for toys. It fueled my imagination. I recall many happy memories of playing outside with my siblings. Was our life perfect? No. But, it set the landscape for who I am today and provided the tools I needed to embrace my journey.

When I was a child, our family would get into my father's Chevy van, and he would take us for a Sunday drive. We drove through the countryside, soaking up the sunshine and breathtaking views. Now and then, we'd stop to enjoy a picnic on our way to the natural spring where we collected our drinking water when our well went dry.

Nobody made better sandwiches than my parents. These double-deckers were always a deli feast on a hearty roll. So thick, you had to eat them with two hands. Inside, Italian meats and cheeses, and garden lettuce and tomatoes. It was a culinary masterpiece.

My friends didn't care about the country drives, but the sandwich was hard to resist. Likewise, I coveted every word of the amusement park stories my friends told and counted the days when I'd start "my" big city life. Later, I discovered real riches aren't in shopping malls and worldly entertainment. My early memories taught me the true riches in life are laughter, family time, and good friends.

We found joy in big family gatherings and celebrating holiday traditions. Sunday supper was at 2 o'clock and included extended family. Summer meant playing with our cousins and riding horses. We had regular sleepovers at my grandparent's house, where it was always a party. I'm not sure which caused more excitement, not having a bedtime, or eating dessert before dinner.

My parents grew our food, and we never went hungry. A woodstove stocked with firewood kept us warm in winter. I never remember feeling cold.

I've grown to appreciate the simple things in life. The beauty of blossoms, newly fallen snow, a child's smile… Special moments make an abundant life. We often miss these moments while waiting for the big things to knock on the door. Sometimes, we're stuck waiting.

"Where are we going?" I always wanted to know everything. I was the self-appointed "know it all," trying to convince everyone I knew a tad more than my younger siblings.

"Old Man Bill's," my father replied. We squealed with delight and jumped in our seats as he slid the door shut on the blue van.

Elderly people have always fascinated me, and I preferred their company to most kids my age. Mr. Bill was one of the happiest old fellows I had ever met. He always wore a big straw hat to protect his bald head from the scorching sun. Mr. Bill also had a large tumor on the back of his head. He revealed it on accident one day when his hat tipped forward, and we all saw the apple size mass peeking out at us. We didn't ask him what it was or how he got it. But, our rides home included a chorus or two of "It's Raining, It's Pouring."

We arrived, and my father parked in front of the old barn and shut off the engine. I pulled open the sliding door, and we all jumped out of the van, ready to make a quick dash to Mr. Bill's front door. He always knew when we were coming and waited at the edge of the dirt and gravel driveway. His big toothless grin left no doubt he was happy to see us. One of us would report if the top pocket of his faded denim overalls was bulging. It was a pocket we knew well.

Our parents didn't allow us to eat many sweets, except for holidays, but they always made an exception at Mr. Bill's.

"Ready for the circus?!" Mr. Bill said in his country drawl. He leaned toward us and pulled out the gigantic pale orange candy. We tried to stay still but could hardly do it. We fidgeted with anticipation, giggled, and held our hands wide open as we waited for him to drop a few soft, chewy morsels into our palms.

True to our childish natures, our mission was to get as much candy as our mama would allow. We were ready to fill our pockets but had nothing to give. But my dad had another idea. He wanted us to offer our friend something money can't buy; friendship.

God doesn't provide gifts so we can live extravagant, pampered lives. He gives so we can be givers, sharing everything, our money, our time, and our talents. To fill hearts with the love of God as we become the hands and feet of Jesus, the quintessential giver.

A few years ago, I realized a special gift. While walking my dog, I glanced back at my tiny house. The moon was bright; the stars glistened like diamonds against the black sky. It seemed as if the porch light beckoned, I AM A BLESSING. I stood motionless as tears dripped off my chin. God showed me I was complaining about the size of my home, yet to someone, this house was a mansion. Still, I need a bigger house, but I'm thankful God has been generous and has given me much more than I deserve.

I'm not sure what Mr. Bill would think of my tiny house. He lived alone in a little shack with no running water or telephone. This mountain man worked the land

and sold a few eggs and vegetables to fill the gas tank of his rusty pickup truck. I suspect he didn't get many visitors. And circus peanuts must have cost him a fortune on his limited income. Our visits to him were random, but we always hoped the long journey would end in sugar.

Mr. Bill savored our Sunday visits as much as we wished to peek in his pocket. His fading blue eyes still sparkled as he shared those circus peanuts. For candy, we gave up our Sunday to give an elderly man our time and friendship. I believe we blessed him, and he blessed us.

Old Man Bill gave a gift only God can allow us to see. We saw a glimpse of pure joy. Mr. Bill's inner happiness had nothing to do with earthly riches. He had a thankful heart.

It's never too late
to share your gifts
and talents.

Sometimes, we're going through something so overwhelming we have nothing to give. We feel drained. That's when God will provide us with the grace that enables us to be givers. To bless someone else is a gift we can give ourselves during a season of spiritual or emotional drought. A kind gesture can transform someone's life and our own.

Latosha Frye gave a fruit cup to a homeless man. His reaction inspired her to establish the Roman's Gift Project. RGP cultivates the power of community giving, through awareness and holistic outreach programs. Volunteers make and distribute her Hope Bags to the homeless population.

Service brings meaning to our lives. It is a way to restore joy to others while we refill our souls.

As Mark Twain said, "To get the full value of joy, you must have someone to divide it with."

"Give, and it will be given to you: good measure, pressed down, shaken together, and running over will be put into your bosom. For with the same measure that you use, it will be measured back to you." Luke 6:38

PRAYER:

Father, I thank You for the many gifts and talents You have given me. Thank You for showing me that the most precious gifts are not those that the world recognizes. Open my eyes so I can see real gifts through Your eyes. Show me how I may share my gifts to make someone's world a little brighter today.

In Jesus' name. Amen.

Reflection

Think about your gifts. What can you give? Is it resources or time? Can you nurture a friendship? Even a cheerful spirit is a gift God might call you to share. Pick something and give it away.

_____

_____

_____

_____

_____

_____

_____

Remember a unique gift that arrived suddenly. How did you feel?

_____

_____

_____

_____

_____

_____

_____

Recall a time when you blessed someone? What happened when you surprised them?

_____

_____

_____

_____

_____

_____

_____

_____

The Bible says it is more blessed to give than receive. Why is that?

_____

_____

_____

_____

_____

_____

_____

_____

Journal your story

Chapter 2

ARE YOU GOING TO WEAR THAT?

~~~~~

'm embarrassed to say people have asked me this question far too often. I thank them. Most folks didn't have the nerve to ask.

I wore a pair of shiny black spandex pants for way too long when it was no longer stylish. The 80s trend brought big permed hair, skin-tight jeans, and shimmering shirts. I'm mortified as I recall myself parading as the Pied Piper of that awful fashion trend. I'd embellish my outfits with a 3-inch wide black belt and 5-inch pumps. I would wear an outfit like this to the club, or anytime I wanted to appear well dressed. Even a random shopping trip. _What was I thinking?_ Now, I laugh at my raw fashion sense in those early years. Much of this adorning was birthed out of self-doubt.

My longing to please everyone led me to overdress. I wore an old prom dress to a wedding. Except for the bridesmaids, not one woman sported a floor-length gown. Decked out in the wrong color, I couldn't resist showing off on the disco floor, flipping my waist-length hair. There, I learned how to dance in a long dress but had a heck of a time keeping my spiked heels out of the hem. Truth disclosure, this habit of dressing mayhem goes way back.

In grade school, my first communion dress captivated my passion for fashion. I should have never worn this anywhere outside the church. This outfit was way too fancy for school; it had a formal ritual written all over it. I didn't care. I could have slept in that dress if my mother let me. It was the most beautiful dress I owned. In the privacy of my room, I wore it, spinning around and dancing like Cinderella. It became a Halloween costume when I wanted to pretend I was royalty.

The most outrageous wardrobe decision was the day I wore my communion dress to school. At times, my mother tried to protect me from embarrassment. This wasn't one of those times. Oh, I wish she would have brought out the big guns and said, "NO, you may not wear your communion dress to school!"

Instead, she gave me the official, okay, and I wore head to toe gleaming white and lace on a regular school day. Maybe, the white gloves tipped them off, but the mean kids wasted no time to ask the teacher, "Why is she wearing a wedding dress to school?" I'm not at all surprised why I can't remember crawling back to school the next day, but I'm sure I did.

Sadly, I believed a new dress would make me more popular. I wanted to sparkle, and I thought a glitzy outside might make my classmates want to know me better. I didn't even know me. I couldn't find myself, let alone expect anyone else to. Even at a young age, I hoped to gain acceptance by what I believed the world wanted me to be. I'm thankful for the handful of people who loved me, anyway.

Eventually, I passed all my frilly dresses to my baby sister, who took her turn playing the princess game.

There is a photo of her flashing a broad, toothy smile while wearing one of her favorite hand-me-down dresses. It was a beautiful blue party dress, trimmed with white lace. We were all clueless; it didn't cover her behind and we never knew it should.

Early on, I discovered popularity had no protocol. It wasn't the dress which made the child. Popular girls were not always attractive or thin. They didn't always wear what I thought was a great outfit. They let their flaws show. But that didn't keep me from trying to cover mine.

Even in youth, these girls demonstrated poise and confidence. Genuine authenticity comes from knowing and accepting ourselves as God made us.

Over the years, I've learned to stop dressing to impress. Watching mouths drop while I paraded through a room in the wrong outfit was more than uncool, it was awkward. It gets expensive to wear new clothes and jewelry every time you meet your gal pals for lunch. And it's not the best way to keep friends.

Failing to see any results from my efforts confused me. When dressing up didn't get me the attention I craved, my mission became to de-sparkle. A Giants sweatshirt and a pair of faded Abercrombie & Fitch jeans became my new favorite outfit. Around the house, cleaning or shopping, and even a lunch date with my friends. Photo albums show me eating, living, and sleeping in the same sweatshirt. Confidence does not mean we stroll around like a disheveled mess. That, too, will push people away.

Dressing to impress reminds me of car shopping. We check out the shiny, decked out car, only to discover a few controls don't work, and we're disappointed. Or we walk past another vehicle that sparkles so much we assume it's out of our league.

And there's another car, a filthy car so full of flaws we don't take it for a test drive. We avoid the dirty car, but under the dirt might be all the features we wanted.

We test-drive the decent looking car that proves to live up to its claims after we've looked under the hood and stepped inside.

An *aha* moment was the day I grasped God already made me fit for this world. As me. When we're authentic, life clicks, and the right people show up.

Our outward appearance is our strongest advertising. We are revealed in the transparency of our smile and our vulnerability. When we relax, take off our mask, and lay it all out, the good, the bad, and the ugly, that's when the sparkle comes out. We project an image that seems real, even with a close-up view.

Now, I've adopted a signature look for each occasion in my life. The lesson I've learned about dressing is, if I'm worried about my attire, it's time to look in the mirror. Most often, it means I'm trying to be someone I'm not.

Walt Disney once said, "The more you are like yourself, the less you are like anyone else." When I'm at ease with myself, that's when I can relax around others.

It's never too late
to discover the
authentic you.

I love the word authenticity. It spells excitement and is filled with energy and enthusiasm. Authentic people own everything God made them be. A person is not only aware of their imperfections but embracing them. You accept who you are and proudly offer your gifts to the world. You show up as yourself. You don't need approval to be you.

Henry David Thoreau said, "Be yourself, not your idea of what you think somebody else's idea of yourself should be."

Authentic people are vulnerable. They share their fears and weaknesses. We are comfortable with these people because they do not pressure us to be perfect.

As no two fingerprints are alike, there is no one else in the universe created like you. Only you can fulfill the destiny prepared for you. Everything is laid out before you. Why be a second-rate copy of someone else when you can rock the world as yourself? Be authentic.

"I will praise You, for I am fearfully and wonderfully made; Marvelous are Your works, and that my soul knows very well." Psalm 139:14

PRAYER:

Father, I thank You for making me the way I am. If I remain as You created me, I will attract all the right people into my life. Help me remember that I need not change myself or be someone I'm not. Everything You've given me, my looks and my personality is one of a kind, and made for a purpose. Help me stay on track being who I am, so I don't miss the blessings in store for my authentic self.

In Jesus' name. Amen

Reflection

When do you feel most authentic?

_____

_____

_____

_____

_____

_____

_____

_____

How do people respond when you reveal your most genuine self?

_____

_____

_____

_____

_____

_____

_____

_____

Describe a time you chose an outfit inappropriate for the situation.

_____

_____

_____

_____

_____

_____

_____

_____

Can you remember a time you tried to be someone you weren't? What happened?

_____

_____

_____

_____

_____

_____

_____

Journal your story

Chapter 3

CRACKED, BUT NOT BROKEN

~~~~

The car screeched as it slid across the pavement and came to a complete stop. The odor of burnt rubber filled the air, but it was too late.

My dad sprinted toward the road, and we all followed. We stopped at the end of our driveway and saw the brown and white fur in a puddle of crimson blood.

"Is he dead?" we shouted. All us kids stood on tiptoes at the end of the driveway, craning our necks to get a better look while our mother held us back. We didn't step one inch beyond the gravel, even then.

"No. Not dead," my father shouted as he pulled our dog from the sticky mess marking the spot where Ringo had met his match.

Before I'd met Ringo, I thought I liked dogs. The evidence is in the photos of me and my grandparents smiling as we played with cute, friendly, cuddly lap dogs. Dogs slathering me in sweet puppy love and sending me into a frenzy of giggles.

Ringo was different. He joined our family when I was four years old. There was a big difference in his demeanor compared to other dogs I had met. Ringo talked with his teeth.

As a toddler, I remember my feet came near the edge of the couch. When my mom propped us up on the sofa like porcelain dolls in a toy store window, I was the only one that missed the safe zone. My siblings giggled as they watched my bare toes stick out for Ringo's nipping pleasure. Ringo was a big puppy with big paws, and as the oldest of my siblings, I was still small. My encounters with this dog altered my view of canines for a long time.

Ringo got all the right chromosomes, which made him a breed of schizophrenic mongrel. He was part German Shepherd and part who knows what. He did commit to keeping our household safe and alerted us to stranger danger on the horizon. The caveat was that his methods were unreliable, and no amount of scolding would keep him at bay.

When I was in the first grade, our family moved to a 20-acre property set back from the road. It was a relief to learn Ringo would no longer stay inside. But he roamed free outside, which was my playground, too.

At night, he was an ideal watchdog. But, his daytime tactics were a little intimidating, scaring away strangers and our friends. Visitors were few after my father posted the official warning… *Beware of the dog!* Ringo never stopped barking, chased people on foot, and to our dismay, even cars.

The crazy mutt would dash out after each vehicle as they sped down the country road. Up and down hills, corners, and curves, Ringo would chase them until they raced out of sight. Each time he chased away the peril, he would trot back, ready for another mission. Reprimands bounced off him like an oiled duck.

At night, he sat outside, guarding our front door. The country night is much darker than a city night. He kept us safe. During the day, his protective nature morphed him into a scary wild animal. As a child, I absorbed his outbursts like a loofah. My father seemed to like this dog more than us kids. Ringo nipped at my feet, killed my cat, and bit my friend on the butt for handing my mother an egg, yet he still had a home with us. I hated dogs. Ringo taught me the truth about canines. Dogs were mean, and I shivered whenever he came close.

Although I didn't want this dog in my life, I did not want him splattered on the road either. But, this event was a turning point, Ringo had chased his last car.

After being hit by the car, he had a broken leg, which healed in a stiff V-shape, making him the ridicule of onlookers. My dad, a loyal dog master, loved him anyway.

Ringo walked around on three good legs and a war trophy sticking out of his side. Broken limbs weren't enough to deter this dog from chasing cars. Soon, the pursuit was on.

Ears flapping in the wind as he chased each car and truck brave enough to drive past our house. He ran even faster as if to get back at them for breaking his leg.

On Sunday evening, we sat on the front lawn: my parents, us kids, and Ringo. As cars drove by, despite my father's command, the maniac dog would dash out after each one. He barked and ran alongside the passing vehicles until he chased them out of sight. Then, we'd see "Hop Along" trotting back, and smiling in dog lingo as if to say, "Got another one pops!"

Aren't people much like Ringo? Even when life has broken our leg, we aren't ready to surrender. We crawl back to what hurts us. It comes in incognito, but we sniff it out. We're captivated by what we should have learned is to be off-limits.

Sometimes, it's a habit, or a person drawing us back. It often takes more than a broken leg for us to get it.

If we're lucky, we might end up with only broken legs. Or, we may lose much more than we were ready to give up. And, I've been there more often than I care to admit. I'm not complaining. Thank God, I'm discovering how to learn from my past without living there. In my twenties, questions were tough to invite into my heart, and it was even harder to hear the answers. The truth scared me. I'm braver now.

Poor Ringo never got over the allure of gas fumes and shiny, spinning hubcaps. His misdirected commitment to what was wrong for him cost him his freedom. Bound by his desire, he spent the rest of his life living in a fenced area my father prepared for him.

It's fascinating we often choose a penned in life even when we see a clear path. Standing at the crossroads, we contemplate the familiar over the unknown. We lean toward what we know for sure. Even to the extent of allowing people to chart our path and define our future instead of taking chances.

I've learned to accept cold hard facts about myself. I'm learning change *is* good. Bravery is being afraid and doing it anyway. And sometimes, it's necessary to cut losses and give up the worry about the wasted time invested into chasing *that thing*. Turn and make a new investment.

It's never too late
to step outside your
comfort zone.

I enjoyed the movie *50 First Dates* starring Adam Sandler and Drew Barrymore. Drew's character had lost her short-term memory. Lucy would wake up with no memory of the previous day, except for celebrating her father's birthday. Each night, her family would reset the stage so she would wake up to relive that day. They were careful not to miss a single detail. Each day she picked out the same clothes and read the same newspaper, drove to the restaurant and ate the same meal. They ate birthday cake every day.

Some people live the same day repeatedly. That's like living in your comfort zone every single day. I'm guilty of getting trapped there myself, sleepwalking through life where nothing changes. It's the same day, different year, endless mediocrity. It gets worse. Some folks do it again, even when it feels wrong. I've taken a more daring approach and explore my days more purposely now. Spend your days wisely. Join me in doing the opposite of what you would usually do today and look for a blessing. Take a different route to work. Try a new food for lunch. Join a group. Learn something new. Whatever is keeping you from living a new day, step outside your comfort zone and grasp it. But whatever you do, remember life is too short to live the same day twice. From the wisdom of Alfred Tennyson, "The shell must break before the bird can fly."

"See then that you walk circumspectly, not as fools but as wise, redeeming the time, because the days are evil. Therefore do not be unwise, but understand what the will of the Lord is." Ephesians 5:15-17

PRAYER:

Father, help me see things as You see them. Give me the courage to stop echoing thoughts that no longer serve my life. Open my eyes to see the splendor You have set before me and the myriad of choices I can make, which will enhance my experience. I want to celebrate the new days and fresh opportunities. Help me see that stepping outside my comfort zone and venturing into the unknown with You is far safer than staying penned in with the familiar. I'm ready to get uncomfortable.

In Jesus' name. Amen

Reflection

What about change scares you?

_____

_____

_____

_____

_____

_____

_____

_____

Is there a decision you're avoiding because fear is parked
at your doorstep?

_____

_____

_____

_____

_____

_____

_____

_____

What's the worst that could happen if you took a risk?

_____

_____

_____

_____

_____

_____

_____

What would you do if you knew you couldn't fail?

_____

_____

_____

_____

_____

_____

_____

Start today!

Journal your story

Chapter 4

BLACK AND BLUE

~~~

As far back as I can remember, it's been difficult for me to say no. That is until I realized my dirty little secret had been germinating in selfish motives.

Cloning myself was a dream birthed of sheer ego because there wasn't enough of me to go around. I believed there wasn't anybody who could do it, let alone do it better. So, I spent years tottering through life like a chimpanzee carrying a monster backpack full of bricks and sinking deeper and deeper into solid cement.

I'm still hiding behind an excuse. But now, my busyness isn't as self-centered, but it has become a distraction for the things I don't want to face. Though I'm not sure it's an improvement, I tell myself I'm maximizing my productivity by doing a lot, all at once. Who am I kidding? I'm only breathing harder.

Often, sleep deprivation hits me so hard I don't sense being tired until I sit for five minutes and wake up pulling my face out of my salad. Is there one woman reading who understands?

My schedule has no buffer. I'm a poster child for dysfunctional work-life balance. I divide my time between important things. Still, essential tasks remain undone at home. My days run together like a freeway lined with closed exit ramps. Each sign depicting the next task on my agenda with no way to onboard and do it. Sometimes, I'm so busy I can't remember enjoying the last thing when it's over. It's no way to live. There are many more improvements to make. Still.

Five minutes lost can wreak havoc in the morning. I've become an expert in the wizardry of rushing. Rushing out the door while brushing my teeth, rushing to put makeup on at stoplights, rushing into the building for a meeting, and landing in my seat two seconds before the meeting starts.

I've struggled to accept that over scheduling may be one of my most significant flaws. It's not enjoyable to do everything at the last minute. But I love so many things. I'm like a kid who can't pick only one. I want them all. Time constraints make you selective. I realize there will never be a way to make a 24-hour day into 36. Still, I try.

Despite all the juggling, I'm organized, at least in my brain. I imagine a precision domino effect that gives me peace. Oh, and if I could live in a perfect world, I'd be unstoppable. *So, what's stopping me?*

There is a legitimate reason I couldn't do it, at least in my mind. There's not enough margin in my day. Yet, my gut tells me I'm prioritizing the wrong things.

"You didn't go to work today?" my husband asked, surprised to find me wearing faded jeans and a t-shirt. *Yes, I know. Who takes a Tuesday off instead of the weekend?*

"I didn't have time. I took a personal day," I said, pulling a load of towels from the dryer.

"You didn't have time? To go to work?" The smirk on his face filled in the blanks.

That's a fair retort. Most folks use personal days to go to the beach, appointments, or to visit out-of-town families. I take a day to catch up on laundry or cash my paycheck… from last month.

It's safe to say I'm like a clown pedaling a unicycle while trying to balance a giant stack of plates in each hand. Does anyone relate? I ride a little, juggle the plates, and move back and forth ever so. I lean this way, and that way, so no dishes hit the ground. But, it's only a matter of time until everything crashes.

To simplify my mornings, I hang out my clothes for the next day by keeping a rotating line of suits on the closet rack. I've even adopted a uniform for simplicity. Everything is black. Sweet and easy. But, it was not always this way; dressing for work.

Why am I telling you all this? Life in the whoosh once left me in an embarrassing situation. I worked in an office building at the top of a high rise. Too lazy to take the stairs, I'd waste an extra fifteen minutes riding along as the elevator made its way to the top and delivered me to my floor.

On this day, I was wearing a new, irresistible black and white houndstooth suit. I collected suits, as some women collect shoes and purses. This one was a cute short jacket and skirt combo. I wore it with a classic white blouse and a pair of pumps. I was sure everyone would like it.

The crowded elevator left me no choice but to stand with my back to the door, facing my colleagues. On Monday mornings, we weren't in a hurry to get off. We all enjoyed a pleasant exchange of small talk and babble about weekend happenings.

It wasn't long before people were watching me and grinning. *Loving my new houndstooth suit.* I stood proudly as a peacock, waiting for someone to ask me where I bought this remarkable suit.

My back ached, and I could sense the misalignment more than usual. Diagnosed with scoliosis in the fourth grade, I learned one leg is a ¼ inch shorter than the other. For years, I wore a lift in one shoe, and this day I hadn't worn it. Aggravated by the shorter leg, I shifted from one foot to the other and leaned against the side of the elevator.

Well, here we were, a dozen of my co-workers and me making spectacles of ourselves stuffed into this glass elevator, and I'm standing front and center facing them all.

When I glance down to the floor, I'm mortified to discover I'm wearing two shoes. Let that sink in for a minute. Two shoes that *don't* match! Not, in style…not in heel height, and not in color.

You could have fried eggs on the heat of my skin, and it glowed 20 shades of red. I glanced back at my feet. How could I sneak off this elevator? Act like it was any other day. *Seriously, who would ask me why I was wearing two color shoes?* I could stand straight and walk off the elevator. Simple. Done deal. *Don't draw attention to yourself, Diana.* It was already too late. Regardless, my colleagues would walk behind me and laugh at me all the way to my cubicle. I couldn't bear to deflect insults and stares all day long. Nine hours was a long time to spend walking around the department in the wrong shoes. Even suitably dressed the next day, it would be hard to face them. I imagined it would be months before the gossip would die down at the water cooler.

Possibly, a great excuse was I *wanted* to wear two shoes of different colors. Isn't any reasonable woman free to wear one black and one navy shoe? With two heel heights?

Or, maybe I left the other black shoe at my desk. And, this event was a shoe swap mission. *So, you left work wearing one shoe?* Nope.

Funny conversations we have with ourselves. Who was I kidding? I would be visible all day, in meetings, at lunch, on breaks, and in the restroom. I could imagine women lined up staring at the bottom of the bathroom stall and asking each other, "Who's the freak wearing two different shoes?"

My colleagues would start a wager, and one lucky winner would earn cold cash for counting the most times they found the thirtysomething fashion geek wearing one black and one blue shoe. A corporate spin on Where's Waldo.

I saw one way out. So, I laughed. Hard and loud, belly laughs. Right there in the elevator. I looked at everyone and said, "You won't believe this! I'm wearing two different shoes!" I howled again.

People tell me my laugh is infectious, which proved correct when everyone joined the laughing spree. Soon, the elevator was roaring with laughter. It was empowering. Instead of everyone laughing *at me*, everyone laughed *with* me. I explained my mishap, and for the rest of the day, I milked every opportunity to laugh at my mistake. It was easy to do because I spent most of the day in stocking feet, which led to the question, "Where are your shoes?"

"Well," I said, repeating the entire scenario. I still chuckle about it.

I'm not cured. I still rush around. I multi-task and try to handle too much. I'm notorious for dressing mishaps; unzipped pants, shirts inside out, a static knee-high hanging on the back of my pant leg, different socks…the list goes on.

Okay, it's my fault. I create my schedule. But I'm showing progress. I'm building margin into my calendar; still, I might need a personal assistant.

I'm learning to relax and let go. Sometimes I reject the good for the better. Or, maybe I must free up an extra five minutes to find my shoes.

It's never too late to relax and let it go.

Women are always doing too much. We wear an arsenal of hats and try to be the best at all our jobs. Often, we are doing the wrong jobs or not prioritizing. Sometimes my life is akin to a hamster wheel, round and round I go with no end to the tasks at hand.

Not in a man's world. They grab the chips and watch football for hours if it's what they want to do. They don't feel one iota of guilt for wasting time.

End of the year, or end of your life, which of your priority tasks will matter? People will matter. Relationships will matter. The kids might not remember that you were a freak about keeping the dishes clean. But they will remember that they asked you to read them a story, and you were too busy. No one will care if you wait one more day to do the laundry, or if you brought home takeout food instead of cooking.

Make time for you. Stop sweating the small stuff and relax. Ignore the minutia and love your family. The things that matter most need your priority attention. The rest of it will take care of itself.

I read somewhere that "sometimes the best thing we can do is not think, not wonder, not imagine, not obsess. Simply breathe." Catch your breath, sit back. Everything that must work out always does. God's got this.

"If God is for us, who can be against us?" Romans 8:31

PRAYER:

Father, help me see it's not my job to strive. You've laid this day before me, and it's my job to enjoy the journey, living one moment at a time in Your presence. Some things will require Your strength to help me through the day. I trust You have the outcomes determined, and if I lean on You, I need not worry. I need not control every situation, and I need not do everything. With Your help, I can relax and let it go. Your timing will always be perfect.

In Jesus' name. Amen.

Reflection

What makes it hard for you to say no?

_____

_____

_____

_____

_____

_____

_____

_____

_____

As women, we believe we must do it all. Why?

_____

_____

_____

_____

_____

_____

_____

_____

_____

Where should you create more margin in your day?

_____

_____

_____

_____

_____

_____

_____

*If no one questioned you, what would you give yourself
more time for today?*

_____

_____

_____

_____

_____

_____

_____

Do it!

Journal your story

Chapter 5

WOULD YOU RECOGNIZE A LIFEBOAT?

~~~

I read about a lifeguard who punched a drowning man. He explained to the reporters the man was fighting him and to save his life, he had to get him to give up.

Our lives are like this. We think we can do it all, and even when we sink, the struggle continues as we try to keep ourselves afloat. We don't ask for help; we want to control the outcome. It's no use. We can't stay up without a raft. So, we surrender and wait for the rescue boat.

But would we recognize it when it came? And, when we call for help, do we genuinely _want_ help? I'm inclined to believe we do, but only on our terms. I'm guilty of wanting to call the shots.

"You're going to learn to swim" were unpleasant words to my ears. I peeked out from behind my sunglasses.

My father was not his usual picture of authority. He stood barefoot sporting a visible farmer tan distinct against his pale stomach. A protruding belly barely fitting into his faded denim cut-offs.

Moments before, I had greased myself with baby oil and was enjoying my daily baking ritual as I had done every sunny day since the start of summer. My round red Panasonic radio was blaring my favorite tunes. This was my time. Any manner of getting wet would be more than a minor inconvenience. I had no intention of leaving the comfort of my lounge chair.

"I'm going to—WHAT?" I sprung to a sitting position. Fish swim, turtles swim, but humans are land creatures. No, I would not learn to swim. Not today or any day.

My stubbornness had consequences. While my sister and brother were taking swimming lessons from our father, I was charged with the garden duty, weeding an acre of corn until my fingers bled. Suffocating in dirt was better than drowning.

At the community pool, while my siblings frolicked in the water with their friends, tossing beach balls back and forth, I baked on a lounge chair hiding behind dark sunglasses and a floppy homemade sun hat. I donned a fake smile and continued to replay the spiel about how much happier I was playing sun goddess and reading a book. I lied.

My fear of water diminished two years later, after I got an honorary dunking thrust upon me, courtesy of my well-meaning best friend. My boring escapades drained Janie. Or perhaps she tired of the attention they took from her, but whatever the reason she coerced me into the shallow end of the pool where she demanded I dunk myself in the water. We weren't leaving until I did.

Dunk me? Did she mean, submerge me? In water, as in getting my hair wet? My ponytail was a horsetail and would take hours to dry even in the sun.

"I can't do it," I whispered, shaking as if I were standing naked in a pool of ice water on a snowy day. Witnesses chanted snide encouragement as they lined up around the swimming pool.

"Yes, you will." Janie said with the authority of one teacher who would grab a kid by the collar and march them to the principal's office. She had the power of persuasion. I always buckled under a dollop of her peer pressure. This time more embarrassed about not doing it than afraid of doing it.

Slower than a turtle, I lowered myself into the water, holding my nose as she gave my head a firm push. If something might snap my neck, I was sure this was it.

I popped out of the water, gasping for air like a drama queen while boasting about my underwater adventure. Head to toe, I was sopping wet. Meanwhile, my peers had lost interest and were busy doing somersaults off the diving board.

I continued to brag of other lame achievements, like walking to the deep end in the water below my chin. I wore rubber armbands and floated on a raft while wearing a life jacket. Sometimes, I'd hang onto the swimming pool rim and let my legs drift backward. "Look at me!" I was a pathetic 7th grader.

Thank goodness, we outgrow our dorkiness and learn to view the world through a cleaner lens. Those memories remind me that some small things appear far more frightening than they are. Life events, like my pool experiences, bring us face-to-face with the fear of the unknown. What would happen if I tried to learn to swim? I knew people floated. I saw people floating. But, I believed an extra layer of security was necessary to keep me safe in the water. My struggle to control only helped me sink deeper. Peace and freedom came with surrender.

We hear about God's mercy, grace, and forgiveness, but we don't take the time to wrap it around our brains. Is it simple to let go? Will God take over and steer my boat to shore? Or is it reserved for the chosen?

Will He do it? If the mess is big enough, will God need my help? On and on, we ask ourselves.

God is faithful to save. He doesn't need our help to do anything. Often, we have not because we ask not.

*It's never too late
to trust God.*

Worry is the opposite of trust. When we think it will not turn out okay, we fret. We imagine all the scenarios and what might go wrong. We rehearse each scene as if we are sure it will happen. Why else would we imagine countless ways to respond to something that hasn't given us the slightest inkling it might arrive?

Worry is a thief. The phantom ghost of anxiety will steal your joy and peace daily if you let him live in your brain. So, what if next week something happens? Handle it next week, but don't lose the whole week before you must tackle the problem. There is a silver lining beneath every obstacle. If we are open to receive it, the challenge delivers the reward. We'll become better people by having experienced it.

John Mason says, "obstacles will reveal what you truly believe and who you really are. They introduce you to yourself." You get to choose between worry or trust.

Here's a little exercise. Pick up a pencil. Think of the writing instrument as the challenge you worry about. Drop it. Let go of worry and hold on to trust. It's that simple. Once you realize most things you worry about never happen, it gets much easier. Drop your worries like a pencil. Trust God. He has chosen the best life for you, and it will happen.

"Have I not commanded you? Be strong and of good courage; do not be afraid, nor be dismayed, for the Lord your God is with you wherever you go." Joshua 1:9

PRAYER:

Lord, forgive me for my lack of trust. So often, I think I can control it all, but I can't. Teach me how to let go. You will never abandon those who rely on your faithfulness. Help me understand allowing You to take control of my life strengthens me. In my weakness, with You, I am as bold as a lion. Thank You for being with me wherever I go. I trust you.

In Jesus' name. Amen.

Reflection

Describe a time when you needed help but didn't ask for it. What happened?

_____

_____

_____

_____

_____

_____

_____

_____

Recall a time you had to trust someone. How did you feel?

_____

_____

_____

_____

_____

_____

_____

_____

What are the ways God is asking you to trust him?

_____

_____

_____

_____

_____

_____

_____

When are you tempted to stay in control?

_____

_____

_____

_____

_____

_____

What are the steps you must take to surrender your challenges to God?

_____

_____

_____

_____

_____

_____

_____

Journal your story

Chapter 6

FASHION SENSE

~~~

My first corporate job was in a bustling downtown area. I provided secretarial support to several salesmen and the VP of an insurance agency. Although only nineteen, I was sure I had arrived at the plateau of career success.

My former position required everyone to wear a uniform, so I was ecstatic to learn this new post allowed for a stylish new wardrobe. I enjoyed dressing for work. Fashion was my expertise. (I thought.) So, I noted when a male co-worker lacked style.

I watched Donald wheel his mail cart throughout our department. Every day he delivered the postal mail and internal office communications. He always sported a confident, proud smile and seemed eager to greet each member of the team. I found him charming and delightful, but to my shame, I did not treat him that way. Some experiences you regret later in life. This was one time I'm not proud of.

Despite his apparent lack of fashion sense, what piqued my interest in Donald was his approach to life. He seemed worry-free and radiated unspeakable joy. In all appearances, he was a mess. I looked good. I say this not to boast, but to share the shallow nature of my heart. I did not know The Lord. Everything was about me, me, me. I hoped people would see me as flawless, inside and out, which was far from the truth. On the inside, I was a self-doubting hot mess, and my life had no meaning.

Donald was proud of his job. While it was the lowest position in the company and likely, the least paid, Donald took his career seriously. He brought internal mail delivery to a new level of mastery. Donald knew everything about sending and receiving letters and providing envelopes and packaging supplies.

He proved himself a capable and conscientious worker, arrived 10 minutes early, and was the last to punch out at the end of his shift. He never took extra breaks, and unlike most of us, he seemed to stay on task the entire day, busy working and greeting each co-worker with kindness and respect.

Inside his cart, there were boxes, letters, and large manila envelopes. Sometimes, the stack was in epic proportion to his stature as he maneuvered it throughout the narrow paths between our cubicles. I heard the creaky wheels and saw a splash of color around the corner, and I knew he'd be coming our way soon.

"Tina!" I whispered, leaning over the cubicle wall. "Come on over." Seconds later, my friend arrived with a pack of Kool Super Lights (offering me one before she lit one for herself) as she sank into the spare chair in my work area.

In the 80s, we smoked at our desks. Tina and I used many opportunities to enjoy a quick huddle under the guise of discussing an upcoming project while we satisfied our nicotine craving. Today Donald was a project.

"What is he wearing today?" she asked, taking a deep drag off her cigarette.

"You won't believe it. Mixed patterns. Plaid and something... pink," I said while examining my angora sweater for lint. We both sat, legs crossed, circling our feet as we admired our shoes.

Donald had become the highlight of our mornings. We critiqued his peculiar outfits. We were too comfortable expecting something outlandish. His pants were often three inches too short. He'd wear a clashing loud patterned shirt. Unmatched socks and shoes. Each outfit would drum up a talk at the water cooler, or at least a long second glance. Donald had an eclectic style, and every day it was something different.

I've always believed in the value of good counsel, and Donald needed fashion advice. I was ready to offer my services.

Even as an inexperienced young woman, married without children, I thought I knew everything about life. And especially first impressions, so I felt it necessary to prepare myself. *Prepare for what?* I would give up an entire afternoon to get ready for an evening event, four hours to get ready for work, and two hours to go grocery shopping. My rule was: never leave the house without a full face of makeup and don't wear the same earrings twice in one week. To celebrate myself, I'd often buy a brand-new outfit for nearly any occasion.

Tina and I started our jobs around the same time; she arrived before me. It wasn't long before I was enamored with her. She was two years my senior, so I looked up to her as the big sister I never had. Tina reminded me I was raised in a bubble. She was a smart city girl who taught me the ropes on how to survive a career while navigating a downtown parking jungle, and how to dress. She was stylish, and I wanted to sparkle as she did.

"Great outfit, *Donnie*," we mocked in harmony. He always called himself Donald, but we disregarded his wishes and continued to shorten his name. And every day, he overlooked our insensitivity and responded with a warm smile as he thanked us.

We'd spend the next few minutes poking fun at this innocent, kind young man until our supervisor would ask one of us for a file or instruct us to attend to some other routine clerical task.

One day, after Donald had delivered our mail and received our usual bogus compliments, Tina returned to her cubicle. I thought about Donald wearing those horrible clothes. Either he had zero fashion sense, or he was poor. I'm not sure why I cared, but in an awkward moment, I called him back to my desk.

"Donald."

He returned and waited to see if I had a task for him.

Perhaps, he thought I wanted him to mail a package or a letter. He seemed eager to please.

A part-time job at a clothing store didn't make me a fashion expert, but I believed it was my duty to learn why Donald could not dress. I'm not sure if I wanted to help him, or if I was looking for another level to climb in humiliating him, neither of which I'm proud of. But I was confident, I could offer Donald the first-rate glimpse of my take on how to dress with panache.

"Why do you wear clothes that don't match?"

Wow, I told my co-worker he was a horrible dresser. He was, but I never expected I'd say it…out loud. *Who did I think I was?*

At that moment, stupid. This blurt spouted out and dropped to the floor with a thud. I waited for Donald to show himself to be unkind for the first time. What would he say to a rude, self-proclaimed fashion expert?

To my surprise, Donald carried on as he had always done, with love, kindness, and a forgiving spirit. His sparkling blue eyes stared into mine, and he flashed his usual quirky smile. "I buy my clothes at the thrift store so I can give money to people who have no money for clothes."

He turned and walked away. But, he should have punched me in the face, I would have deserved it. Donald's faith produced a sacrificial labor of love.

I've learned we can't judge outward appearances. My heart had significant flaws, yet on the outside, I shined brilliantly. Donald had the best story. Grounded in genuine agape love, his motive was the love he had for all people, even me. This was something I knew nothing about. I was selfish and still teeter-tottering my way into adulthood.

However on track we think we are, imperfections remain camouflaged to our eyes, yet we seem to zone in on everything we see in others.

It was years before I gave up excessive shopping, but Donald's message planted a seed that echoed in my heart. There is more to life than us. When we live for ourselves, we lose. Living for others leads to an abundant life overflowing. We all have more than we need.

Donald taught me "love" is not about how I feel but marked by the genuine compassion and kindness I can offer to others. How do I make them feel? We encourage people by serving them with gifts, time, and resources while projecting a compassionate and forgiving nature.

It's never too late
to forgive.

Thomas Kempis wrote, "Be patient in bearing with other men's faults and weaknesses, for you also have many things that have to be put up with by others."

We forget. In our minds, everyone else needs fixing, but we may need it more. Not the same things, but something. Trivial things offend us. We nitpick the minor annoyances we discover in people. When people hurt us, we nurse the pain. We pull off the scab, lick our wound, bandage it again, but the bleeding never stops.

What if we fixed our thoughts on the perfect One? The sinless One who bore the sins of all. What if we imitated the One who forgave the worst offense in human history?

Jesus said, "Forgive them, Father, they know not what they do." He is also willing to forgive us for whatever we have done. We're not that important to take offense.

Donald modeled forgiveness daily as he surrendered to be the brunt of our jokes. He knew resentment and unforgiveness is a prison. Forgiveness is humbling. When we're forgiven, the easier it is for us to forgive. Be free. Forgiveness is a gift you give yourself.

"Therefore, as the elect of God, holy and beloved, put on tender mercies, kindness, humility, meekness, long-suffering; 13 bearing with one another and forgiving one another if anyone has a complaint against another; even as Christ forgave you, so you also must do." Colossians 3:12-13

PRAYER:

Father, I thank You for Donald and the many other chances You have given me in my life to witness Your example of true love and forgiveness. Help me remember that You are not impressed with our shiny outsides, but what lives deep in our hearts. Grant me a kind forgiving heart that shows genuine compassion for the needs of others. When I'm tempted to worry about my needs, help me see there is always someone else who needs more.

In Jesus' name. Amen.

Reflection

Remember a time when someone misjudged you based on your appearance. How did that make you feel?

_____

_____

_____

_____

_____

_____

_____

When are you most likely to judge people based on outer appearances or circumstances?

_____

_____

_____

_____

_____

_____

_____

_____

Have you ever experienced a situation where you forgave someone who hurt you?

_____

_____

_____

_____

_____

_____

_____

Have you ever held onto unforgiveness?

_____

_____

_____

_____

_____

_____

_____

Journal your story

Chapter 7

THE BETTER GIFT

~~~~~

When Holly confessed, she wanted a typewriter for Christmas, I knew we would be more than best friends, we were soul mates. Every girl was asking for an Easy-Bake Oven, the Talky Crissy Doll, or the Buffy Make-up and Hair Styling set. Holly, like me, loved to read, and now, she wanted a typewriter.

"It's the Royal Sprite model," she said as if it was hers.

"The blue one? With the red knobs?" I said, grabbing both her hands. I wanted the same.

"Yes!" We hugged to celebrate our excitement. I envisioned us sitting side by side, typing poems, and other cool things, like Top 40 song playlists.

Life is unpredictable. Some things turn out far differently than our best-laid plans.

Christmas morning, I waited to receive my Royal typewriter, and to my initial delight, I got a typewriter. But not until further inspection did I discover it was nothing like the beautiful blue Royal, my friend and I admired. Mine was a plastic toy imitation. A child's, Buddy "easy-touch" typewriter.

You bought me a child's typewriter? I was sure my parents saw I was blossoming into adulthood. I was wrong.

After Christmas break, Holly wasted no time to tell me all about the typewriter she got. She handed me a folded piece of paper.

I loved my friend, but it was the *way* she said she got the lovely blue Royal Sprite model that made it worse.

Holly was one of those smart textbook girls. She came from an ideal family, and she wore perfect little cardigan sweaters over starched and pressed white collared blouses. She slipped her feet into polished black patent leather shoes that shined so bright you could check your makeup in them. A small silver barrette held her red bangs off to the side of her freckled forehead. You couldn't hate her if you wanted to. Holly would get the Royal; she deserved it.

I flashed a fake smile and said, "Wow, me too."

Fast forward five years to high school, and all the business majors were competing for two office jobs. The preferred role would report to the principal. The other position would complete menial tasks for the guidance counselor. I got the second job.

I chalked it up to bad luck and pointed everything back to the day I paired up with a machine named Buddy instead of Royal. *Why did I always come in second?* I pretended all was well, but inside I was sorry I didn't get what I wanted.

Back in the counselor's office, Mr. Andrew's assistant pointed to a stack of boxes taller than me. My job was to sort through the papers in each box and file the documents in the proper drawers. An organizing nightmare.

Whatever I didn't finish in one day, would roll over to the next day, and the following, until the project was complete, and I would no longer have a job. And, the girl awarded "the first place" role would continue typing and getting a paycheck until the end of the school year.

I knew I should take my time and enjoy the $40 I'd get every two weeks if this thing would stretch out until summer. The gloom of the tiny room had taken a toll on me. I longed to be in a brighter place where money could not buy happiness. I hated filing.

Chosen as one of two students hired for the only two paying jobs at school was nothing like getting a toy typewriter when you asked for the *real* thing. Too much thinking about yourself and you have mixed feelings even when good things happen.

God has a way of charting our path in the right direction. Sometimes, the wrong thing gets us where we're supposed to go. It's preparing us for something better.

Eventually, I got my first *real* typewriter, but I learned before turning 20, becoming a secretary was the farthest thing from what I wanted to do with my life. Luckily, I took a few side roads, which led me here.

I did not understand why God would instill in me the longing to learn to type. I thank God I learned and am grateful for Buddy, giving me the first glimpse into my future as a writer.

One thing is sure, God loves his children, and He will give none a Royal when the best gift is a Buddy.

It's never too late to accept God's timing.

I often wonder about the things I prayed for and didn't get. Would a domino effect wreak havoc in my life? I should appreciate unanswered prayer. There were many jobs I thought were perfect, which fell through the cracks, but were replaced with the ideal position.

On the flip side, sometimes God answers prayer by giving us an opportunity. There's no guarantee when the doors will open. But they can close if we don't go through them. Often, that leads to regret from missed chances and sometimes, a complete change in the trajectory of our life.

Today be bold as you venture into the next week, month, or year. Relax, trust God, and accept his timing. While we cannot see around the corner, He can. God knows the entire plan and knows when the timing is right.

"For I know the thoughts that I think toward you, says the Lord, thoughts of peace and not of evil, to give you a future and a hope." Jeremiah 29:11

PRAYER:

Father, thank You for knowing me better than I know myself. Too often, I try to manipulate what isn't meant to be and desire what's not good for me. The next time something doesn't happen the way I want it to, help me say, Thank You. Your timing is perfect.

In Jesus' name. Amen.

Reflection

What ended differently than you hoped, but looking back was what you needed?

_____

_____

_____

_____

_____

_____

_____

_____

How did you feel when you were set on one thing, and it didn't end the way you had hoped?

_____

_____

_____

_____

_____

_____

_____

_____

Have you experienced a loss that was a blessing in disguise?

_____

_____

_____

_____

_____

_____

_____

How has God used a disappointment to reveal a silver lining in your life circumstances?

_____

_____

_____

_____

_____

_____

_____

Journal your story

Chapter 8

ARROWHEADS & PAISLEY PANTS

~~~

Fall is my favorite season. I love the clean and crisp air, lower temps, pumpkin lattes, and the soul-stirring sensation something new and exciting is about to happen.

After spending summers living in the country, where few kids lived, I was always ready to start a new school year. While other students complained that summer vacation was way too short and boycotted back-to-school campaigns, I packed my plaid lunch box and waited for the bus long before it arrived. I was eager to get back to the grind with my school friends, many of whom I hadn't seen in three months.

It was the fall in the '60s, an era when public schools had strict dress codes, and for girls, it meant wearing dresses or skirts and blouses. Pants weren't allowed, not even in the bitter cold winter.

On this day, we were taking a field trip to a local vegetable farm where we would hunt for Native American arrowheads and other artifacts that surfaced after farmers plowed the fields. Since we would dig in the dirt, the dress code changed, and girls could wear pants on the trip. I asked my mom if I could wear pants, but she said no, and I understood it loud and clear. NO. *My bare legs would be in the dirt. Weren't mothers supposed to keep kids clean?*

My siblings and I learned early on asking for something was a hapless quest, and most of our inquiries ended in a firm no, even and *especially*, *if* everyone else was doing it. "No, Dad, I would not jump off the bridge, too…"

It always fascinated me to watch the way television families ran their households. The adults on TV communicated much differently than the adults in my life. There was no arguing. They exchanged a saccharin dialogue that resembled a leisurely game of catch. And they encouraged their kids to speak. I wanted to be that parent when I grew up.

Mike and Carol Brady soon became my idols as I watched their thoughtful family conversations allowing the kids to share their feelings. Family decisions required teamwork, and there were delightful discussions where everyone shared expectations, lessons learned, and more.

I must admit, I've always had an innate longing to connect with people. You know, share the good, the bad and the ugly, iron out the rough spots, say what you mean, and end it all with a cozy bear hug. But, these chats were in my head. I appeared aloof, which was a cover because I got a little choked up when it was time to express my needs and innermost desires.

My suppressed craving to articulate words often manifested itself on paper. I believed if my mom knew how I felt, she would understand and wouldn't let me down. Using my best penmanship, I wrote her a carefully planned, but short letter.

Dear Mom. You said I can't wear pants to school. But, I really want to wear pants on the field trip like all the other girls. Love, Diane.

(That's what my mom always called me.)

After I wrote it, I wasn't sure of the best way to deliver the message. I didn't have the guts to hand it to her. I'd never win a debate, and I didn't want her to get mad. I decided she should discover my letter and read it while she was alone, giving her plenty of time to mull it over.

At first, I thought about slipping it on the kitchen counter, or I'd leave it on the table going out the door. Mom was often in the kitchen, cooking, and cleaning. But, what if she didn't plan to cook or clean? She might not stay inside if it was a gardening day.

My options were few. But my mom would visit the bathroom. So, I carefully placed the letter in the center of the toilet seat lid and hurried off to catch the school bus.

All day, I wondered if she would change her mind and believed in my heart, she would. I wanted to be a big shot wearing pants to school. And I knew the field trip would be a lot of fun *if* I were not the only girl in a dirt field holding my skirt between my legs.

The long bus ride home transported me into a cheesy daydream starring my "Carol Brady mom" who would sit with me on the couch and say, "Honey, I read your letter. I am very sorry for not listening to you when you talked about wearing pants. I understand, and I was wrong. If it's important to you, YES, you may wear pants to school!"

I imagined my happy mama handing me the folded stack of trousers, allowing me to pick out my favorite. She'd give me "the but clause," but this is an exception and only this once.

When the bus approached our driveway, we grabbed our books from the overhead compartment and my siblings, and I scurried off the bus. At the front door, we could smell simmering tomatoes and garlic coming through the kitchen window. Inside, our mom was busy at the counter, preparing meatballs. Most days, we'd go off to play outside until dinner, but today I wasn't in a hurry. I wanted a response to my letter.

Silence echoed, and time dragged on as I dawdled in the kitchen. Not one mention of the day.

More silence followed by, "Who wants to pick lettuce from the garden?"

What!? You mean, you read a heartfelt note from your kid, which you found lying on the lid of a TOILET SEAT, and there's no comment?!

Plan B, I didn't have one. How could I start this conversation? What could I say?

"So, um, Mom, did you get the letter I left you this morning?"

"Letter?"

"Um, yeah, I left it on the toilet seat lid."

"You left me a letter on the toilet seat lid? Why wouldn't you hand me the letter? No, I didn't get your letter."

Imagined or real, her response left me with only one thing I could do.

The next day, I picked out a blouse and a skirt and got dressed as usual. My insides were tingling as I traded my school shoes for a pair of sneakers. It wasn't a gym day, and digging in the dirt was one place even my mom knew, was not the place for dress shoes.

I stared at the brown dresser, my sister and I shared. Even opening it would set off an alarm. The drawers often stuck and made a creaky noise when we opened and closed them. The second drawer held my prize. I slowly opened it and saw my favorite pair of auburn-brown paisley patterned pants neatly folded and laying right on top. My aunt had given these as a Christmas present, and I loved them.

Could I do it? Yup. I was about to cross the threshold of obedience. A BIG deal.

I folded the pants several times into a neat square and stuffed them into a bag. I don't even remember what bag, but I remember feeling like a prisoner escaping from jail. My knees were knocking, and my armpits were dripping with sweat.

Would she ask about the bag? If she did, what would I say? What if she made me open the bag?!

After trembling my way to the front door, spewing out a few awkward verbal distractions, I prayed she wouldn't ask me questions that would force me to lie. I hated lying, and it didn't come easy for me. My strategy was leaving out a few parts and hoping she never asked the right questions.

I slipped out the door without raising suspicion and dashed down the driveway, which appeared longer than it did the day before. Even in sneakers, I couldn't run fast enough. My heart was pounding. Oh, how I wanted to be riding the bus sooner than later. I listened as the engine chugged up the hill but not fast enough.

I wanted to turn around to see if my mom was watching. She always sat at the kitchen window drinking tea as we waited for the bus. But, if she pulled open the ruffled white curtain and peeked her head out to gaze at me, it would be only a few minutes before she'd spring open the front door.

She'd holler from the porch, "Diane. Diane! WHAT IS IN THAT BAAAG?"

I stood motionless, staring straight ahead like a startled doe, and to my relief, the bus pulled up. I got on, found my seat, and plugged all the valves back into my heart chamber. And I sat there relieved, thanking God she hadn't asked me about the bag. With the smile of a Cheshire cat, I watched as our house drifted out of sight. I knew it would be smooth sailing for me now. I had done it.

Upon arrival at school, I informed my teacher I needed to change into my field trip pants. I held up my bag, flashing a big cheesy grin. Inside were the pants I had every right to wear. No kid gets out of the house with what they're not supposed to have. *Do they?*

I rushed to the girls' room, changed and stuffed my skirt into the bag, and afterward, shoved the bag into my desk. I looked spectacular in my favorite pair of casual pants. I was free, and for one day, I'd be like the other girls.

I would have gotten away with it had I devised a more elaborate plan. To my surprise, we marched straight from one bus to another and off to our homes. The other girls wearing the pants they had worn to school. And here I was, dressed in a pair of famously colorful paisley pants my mother had told me I could not wear. And my skirt was still at school.

The entire ride home, I slumped in the seat in total anxiety, mortified, not knowing how I would explain this one. Worse, wondering what might become of me? After a productive day, I went from the fame of a rock star to self-effacing, wishing I could jump into anyone's vest pocket and disappear for the rest of the year. My successful mission had backfired with an explosion. I was in big trouble.

I forget the punishment but remember vividly feeling embarrassed and humbling myself to admit I deserved it. I learned dishonesty never pays. Still, if I had to relive the day, with the possibility of digging in the dirt while wearing a skirt, I won't kid you; I'd do it again. Except I'd forget the bag and put the pants on *before* going to school. And I'd run to the bus stop as fast as my little legs could carry me. I'd board the bus *wearing* pants!

Sometimes, it's better to say what you mean and stand behind it because trying to cover and uncover your tracks takes a lot more energy than dealing with it from the onset.

Right or wrong, we reap what we sow, and there are consequences for every decision. I also learned things are better said than read.

It's never too late
to learn from
your experiences.

Everything that happens to us can either break us or lift us. I want to climb higher. I wasn't a good learner and often repeated the same tests. I've survived similar endings, different stories.

In the spirit world, I'm sure the angels can see the big reject stamp on my forehead, noting how often I bounced back to square one. Now, I'm around the board on a few things, I've learned if we embrace every moment, challenge, or experience that comes our way, and ask God what He wants us to learn, He will tell us. I'm getting better at doing that.

My life experiences have taught me valuable lessons. Life is uncertain, but the challenges help us strengthen our faith and character. We learn what we are made of. Sometimes, we don't know how reliable we are until we're faced with adversity. Finding your strength in one challenge is often what gets you through the next ordeal.

Learn from your experiences, take the good but pack up the rest. History has a habit of repeating itself if we aren't careful.

"The things which you learned and received and heard and saw in me, these do, and the God of peace will be with you." Philippians 4:9

PRAYER:

Lord, when I am tempted to manipulate situations for my benefit, help me see that anything I cannot face with honesty is not worth doing. Let me learn from the example of godly people. Genuine peace comes from living rightly within Your will. Help me see You love me no less when I am wrong, but You still want the best for me. Help me learn from my experiences to build my character.

In Jesus' name. Amen.

Reflection

Think about a time when you had to choose between facing something honestly or manipulating it in your favor.

_____

_____

_____

_____

_____

_____

_____

Have you tried to control situations by digging your own path instead of responding to the circumstances as they arrive?

_____

_____

_____

_____

_____

_____

_____

Think of a situation that taught you a lesson you've continued to carry throughout life.

Journal your story

Chapter 9

THE SHORT ONE, PLEASE

~~~~~

People always say the meaning of courage is being afraid and doing it anyway. If that's true, I've been a coward most of my life.

As a child, it was rare if I stepped out of my comfort zone. Part of the time, because my mom didn't let me do anything that scared her, and every other time, I was already scared to death.

I invariably ran a little slower, so I wouldn't trip and fall. I bounced ever so lightly on the trampoline. And I remained near the edge during a dodgeball game. I didn't catch the ball, I turned away from it to protect myself. *Don't hit me.* My mission to avoid physical pain at all costs. On the most challenging gym days, I was the girl sitting on the sidelines with cramps. I'd always find something to soften every blow. This was one day.

"Lower." I squatted beside the bike marking the height and watched as he unscrewed the bolts and lowered the seat once more.

My new shiny blue bike looked spectacular. My grandpa gave all the grandkids new bikes for no reason, so this summer day was better than Christmas. Mine was a Sears cruiser bike with headlights and a rear rack, which made an excellent passenger seat. It was the Cadillac of bikes.

My sister and brother each got a modern, sporty bike with the banana-shaped seat. The sporty bike seemed so much lower to the ground and safer. Easier to control. My bike was the big kid bike. There were days I tried to convince my parents I was almost a grown-up at 12, but this wasn't a day I was yearning for adult privileges. I wanted to be one of the little kids and learn on the smaller bike. It was the safer ride for sure. My bike was way too tall.

"Okay, try it now," my father said, dropping the screwdriver into his toolbox.

"No. It's not low enough. My feet have to touch the ground."

So, I learned to build safety nets to avoid getting hurt. I wanted to plant my feet firmly on the ground and walk away without a scratch.

I'm amazed I ever learned to ride a bike. In the country, there were no sidewalks. My training course was a 20-foot gravel driveway surrounded by cow pastures and woods.

In my mind, I saw myself emerging from underneath a pile of metal after I crashed. I'd pick gravel out of my knees, which would leave pockmarks big enough to hold water.

Clear thinking rarely exists when hiding in corners and looking over our shoulders. Instead, we dream up many scenarios, most never happen.

When things go wrong, we dislike our pain so much, we block it out. Some things you can only live through once, like the time my big toe got caught in the bike spokes. My sister remembers this more vividly than I do. She said it was swollen and looked painful.

How does one get their big toe stuck in the wheel spokes while learning how to ride a bike?

Perhaps, the bigger question is why I was more comfortable riding barefoot than with sneakers?

It's crystal clear I was desperate to control my situation. Did I think I could grip my barefoot toes if anything went wrong? Yep. Manipulation, I learned well.

Time has taught me that the control we think we have is a facade. When we try to control a situation, we get hurt more than if we let go.

I eventually learned to ride my bike, and there was no going back. We had so much fun attaching playing cards to the wheel spokes and transformed our ordinary bikes into a pack of Harleys that echoed through the woods miles away. We rode our "motorcycles" up and down the driveway and made path marks all over the fields.

It's never too late
to give up control.

When I was young, I wanted to rule the world. Well, at least as it pertained to Diana. Over the years, I've learned patience and try to allow life to unfold around me. I walk through life with a lighter grip. I no longer must call the shots, and I don't want to either.

I'm learning other people have terrific ideas. It's liberating to tell your team the expected outcome and let them determine the steps to get there. They might not do it the exact way I would, but it doesn't matter.

We not only need to give up control of our lives but the lives of our grown children. They may make their own mistakes and travel around the mountains they choose. And while I can save them the heartache of a few treks, if they ask me, I will not be a control freak telling them how to live.

Life has a way of softening us and revealing our hearts. There is nothing God would put into your heart He would not bring to pass. Identify your talents and gifts and do something with what you uncover. Maybe, it's a business you can start or a job you should pursue. Commit your plan to God and let Him drive.

"Commit your plans to the Lord, and your plans will succeed." Proverbs 16:3 NIV

PRAYER:

Father, give me faith to allow You to control my life. Only when I act fearlessly and step out of that fear will You take over. If I manipulate things to remain in power, it only leads to missed opportunities and hurting myself. Today I give You control of my life. Uncover any areas I'm clinging to.

In Jesus' name. Amen.

Reflection

*When are you least likely to trust and want to control
your situation?*

_____

_____

_____

_____

_____

_____

_____

_____

*Are you tempted to give God partial control of any area
of your life? If so, in what area?*

_____

_____

_____

_____

_____

_____

_____

There is freedom in letting go. Where do you need to lessen your grip on a situation?

_____

_____

_____

_____

_____

_____

_____

_____

Journal your story

Chapter 10

WHO STOLE MY FRUIT?

~~~

People say a good therapist can change your life and help you see things differently. I can attest to this. My best friends have always served me well. Included in the happiest chapters of my life is at least one gal pal, or guy, smarter than me, going places, and living life without shades. The daring friend who would let me take off my mask and dart around in a brightly lit room, naked. There, I could share my deepest fears, silly desires, hopes, and dreams in a safe environment without worrying one bit about the color of my outfit. This was one day at Starbucks.

"I expected it to turn out completely different." The monotone in my voice gave no inkling of the back story. I stared into my Café Americana before taking a long, satisfying sip.

"Different? Turn out how—like what?"

"Everything." My response hinted a tinge of regret.

"I hear remorse." Vicki always steered me to reflect on the core of every problem. She was a realist. Unlike me, Vicki had no romantic interpretation of life. She was jaded, and everything was black or white. I see a lot of grays. I don't like the words always and never. She often had an answer. For me, I've learned that sometimes there isn't an answer. But she was about to reveal something that I hadn't thought about.

"Are you concerned that your life seems different from the way you figured it should be? Or is it you haven't come to the defining moment where you're willing to accept the twists and turns of your life?"

I had to admit good questions. I often wondered if I ended up *here* because I went *there*? Or would I have ended up here despite myself because it was destiny?

Maybe, the problem was not one or the other, but I didn't pick either. Instead, I hovered between each, always wondering, *what if?* I was living in perpetual limbo, mentally.

"Both," I said. I knew the final decision would be mine, so why wasn't I making it?

I find it almost comical how some of us (not all) get more indecisive as we age. I'm like that squirrel trying to cross the street, going back and forth. Sometimes, making it, sometimes not. My indecision is often because I know I have far less time to make mistakes. I want to get it right! We all take our first steps as adorable children who have a flawed, but a picture-perfect vision of the future. When I grow up, I will have, and I will be… period.

We grow up and compromise.

The "I will be" career train turned out near the way I imagined. I dreamed of being a photographer and did it. I wanted to write, and I'm doing that. I wanted to be a teacher, and the kind Lord has allowed me to do that as a Sunday school teacher, Girl Scout leader, and manager in various roles.

Regardless of the season, I've always loved my day jobs. Each has afforded me a flexible schedule, autonomy, and use of my left and right brain. My responsibilities have been so enjoyable I would do any of them for free. And I often do these days, resulting in an honorary membership to Workaholics Anonymous. Yet, it's not quite the life I've dreamed about.

And perhaps, it's the reason, the "I will have" train is a different story. If you're a type-A workaholic, you can gain a lot of things you want, but not everything. You miss out on the most important things. I struggle with this and wonder if I got off the workaholic train, would I be able to enjoy my children more, even 2,000 miles away.

All I ever wanted was a family. In my treasure trove of memories, lay flicks from my past. The reruns I cuddle are those that include time spent with close family and friends, the people in my inner circle who touched my heart and dug deep down into the core of my real being. Brave souls who weren't afraid to bring a shovel to Starbucks.

My biggest win was never a promotion; it was planning a fabulous party for my kids and making Mickey Mouse pancakes, or picking up kids from school. Family always came first. Even if it meant moving 2,000 miles across the country for one, and staying a decade too long for another, I would sacrifice my needs for my child.

I planned to keep the fruit of my womb as a part of my daily routine. Even after my kids left the nest, I'd be the mom who kept them well fed. Care packages stuffed with homemade goodies and cartons of spaghetti sauce would be waiting for them to pick up on their way home from work.

Or, I'd do their laundry, or help their kids with a show-n-tell project. I had a plan.

It never occurred to me that my children would design their own life plan in a city nowhere near the place I had landed. *Was my parachute misdirected?*

Kids grow up and stop needing you. Soon, the fruit disappears, and you're left with an empty fruit bowl. We try to prepare for this, but nothing is foolproof. You think you're ready, but you're not. Ever.

As an empty nester, I'm struggling. I must put something first. Without children at home, it's been work.

"Vicki, I miss the ordinary things," I continued. "Young moms talk about how they can't wait to get a break. They're tired. They want time for themselves. I tell them, in 20 years, these days will be the ones you long for."

"So, tell me about the days *you* long for." By now, she was filing her nails, half tuned out, while I was getting way too comfortable on the brown leather sofa, spilling my guts before a dozen coffee drinkers who pretended not to listen.

"I want to indulge in silliness again! Laugh for no reason. Read a dog-eared picture book and enjoy it as if for the first time. Hug my kids, pray with them, tuck them in. Do craft projects. Prepare snacks for after school. Mickey pancakes. Zoos. Sponge Bob. Singing into a hairbrush or imitating Elmo. Pool parties...."

I took a break from the long-winded dialogue knowing she wouldn't be apt to get a word in edge-wise, and continued in a slower, softer pitch.

"I miss the sweet days of doing nothing at all but being with my kids. Savoring those precious moments engaged great conversations about nothing in particular."

She didn't respond. I wondered if she even heard me. I wanted to scream, *Are. You. Listening?!*

The friend with an arsenal of shovels parked beside the table had zoned out on my incessant rant. Where was her famous speech? "Only you can change it."

She filed her last nail, set the nail file on the coffee table and leaned forward, and looked me square in the eye.

"As you look back, dreaming of a former life, are you missing the one you're living in—NOW?"

BAM. Touchdown. And I thought she wasn't even in the game.

I hated she was right. How much time did I waste indulging in sadness because my kids grew up? I'm entering a new season I must enjoy and embrace. Perhaps, I was sacrificing the present days for the former. Sure, I miss my kids, but it won't make them little again. To love them now means letting them find happiness in the lives they have and being glad for them while I build a comfortable living for myself.

Vicki helped me to see I became a workaholic to stifle the loss of my children. Something is comforting about not having time to feel sorry for yourself.

Instead of working to stifle loneliness, getting absorbed in something I've always wanted to do would be a better use of my energy.

Life is full of surprises. At the end of each chapter, it's not what happened in our lives, but the way we responded to the events that matter most. I can sit and wallow over the chapters that turned out differently than I had hoped, but it wouldn't add to my "book."

I started a writer's group to spend time with other writers who share my passion for God and words. This year, I helped other writers get their books in print. I sense this chapter will be more fun than I imagined.

Nothing is better than God steering my boat. It's time to relax! Which reminds me, it's a great time to write another book.

It's never too late
to seize new
opportunities.

Do you see a glass as half-full or half-empty? If you said half full, you're likely to see more to gain than to lose. Life seems to point us in the right direction by revealing to us what's working and what's not.

John Mason says, "You will never see the sunrise by looking to the west. Opportunities can drop in your lap if you have your lap where opportunities drop."

Where we find success will build on our God-given natural talents, gifts, and strengths. Opportunities are everywhere! Ralph Waldo Emerson said, "God hides things by putting them near us." Often, the best chances are right in front of us, but we are looking somewhere else. If you view each experience as an opportunity, then you'll recognize the benefits before hardship.

Faced with recent national tragedies, love knocked at the door, bringing Americans together for a common purpose. Those who didn't see eye to eye laid down their differences and became solutions for those who were desperate.

Unfortunately, the crisis never comes with a warning. We can't waste time in the past or look toward a future that might not exist. What we have is today. And if today you are compelled to choose, or step out and seize something, do it. Tomorrow might be too late.

Let your heart lead you and live to the fullest.

"Do not boast about tomorrow, for you do not know what a day may bring forth." Proverbs 27:1

PRAYER:

Father, I am guilty of having it all worked out and seem derailed by the twists and turns of my life. Every corner brings new opportunities and possibilities but also challenges and lessons to learn. Help me stop living in the past and the future. Today is a gift with opportunities to seize. Open my eyes so I will see all the blessings You have offered me. Give me the courage to accept every day with love and gratitude. Each day is beautiful.

In Jesus' name. Amen.

Reflection

When were you stuck in the past?

_____

_____

_____

_____

_____

_____

_____

How did you let go?

_____

_____

_____

_____

_____

_____

_____

How can you live more fully in the present?

_____

_____

_____

_____

_____

_____

_____

Are there opportunities you can seize by walking in faith?

_____

_____

_____

_____

_____

_____

_____

Journal your story

Epilogue

~~~

The course of life will take you through many seasons bringing with it a mix of joy and sadness, challenges, and times of celebration. There is no journey more important than your spiritual journey. God promises to lead and give us abundant life. He instructs us how to have the best experience here on earth and how to prepare for eternal life. It's all freely offered, and all we must do is accept this gift.

If you haven't allowed God to navigate your life, I encourage you to place your trust in Him. The Lord promises if we draw near to Him, He will draw near to us. He is as close as we want Him to be. As you walk with the Almighty, you will grow more rooted in faith, and your awareness of God's blessings will surround you. You'll gain peace you won't understand and find strength in your weakest moments.

Life is not always comfortable, but our yoke is light in Him. There will be peace in the storm. Jesus gives us the perseverance to press on and to overcome challenges.

If you have never placed your trust in Jesus Christ, I invite you to read the Roman Road. God has a plan for your life, and he's ready to reveal it if you let Him. Call on Him with a sincere heart, and He will listen and embrace you with open arms.

The Roman Road

"As it is written, there is none righteous, no, not one."
Romans 3:10

"For all have sinned and fall short of the glory of God."
Romans 3:23

*"For the wages of sin is death, but the gift of God
is eternal life in Christ Jesus our Lord."*
Romans 6:23

*"But God demonstrates His own love toward us,
in that while we were still sinners, Christ died for us."*
Romans 5:8

*"That if you confess with your mouth the Lord Jesus
and believe in your heart that God has raised
Him from the dead, you will be saved."*
Romans 10:9

*"For with the heart one believes unto righteousness,
and with the mouth confession is made unto salvation."*
Romans 10:10

"For whoever calls on the name of the Lord shall be saved."
Romans 10:13

About the Author

~~~

Diana grew up on twenty acres near a small town in upstate New York, in a neighborhood where she says there were mostly cows and few people. Her favorite pastime became reading or writing poems at an old rock wall. There, she would sit on the hilltop for hours, thinking about the stories she would one day write.

Fast forward a couple decades and God would allow her to propagate her wild writing roots in the west before replanting her back in the east where she worked as a journalist for several newspapers, published her first magazine articles and an e-Book, and later, a cookbook, *Authentic Southern – Recipes, Traditions & Stories.*

She has been a featured writer and copywriter for over 15 years. Her favorite topics to write are Christian living, devotionals, lifestyle, career, travel, history, and cooking.

Diana has contributed to more than a dozen books. She works with authors, entrepreneurs, and job seekers to develop marketing and promotional copy, and has coached first-time authors to write their own books.

She recently authored two titles soon to release. *He Spoke: A Memoir of Grace,* and *Celebrations of Praise: 365 Ways to Fill Each Day with Meaningful Moments.* Her books are available through Amazon and Barnes & Noble.

CPSIA information can be obtained
at www.ICGtesting.com
Printed in the USA
BVHW031847190321
603036BV00009B/212